READINESS FOR RECONCILIATION
A Biblical Guide

Preface

This workbook is designed to assist persons assess their readiness for reconciliation in the midst of conflicts and disputes.

These studies are not intended to provide answers for the dispute itself, but to assure that we are open to God's direction in our lives, open to the healing of relationships and open to the presence of His peacemaking spirit in our turmoil.

Each study consists of some simple yet powerful Scriptures and some questions for you to answer. Do not simply read the questions: take time to write out answers. Memorize the Scriptures, and take these studies seriously. Let this be an instrument for your readiness to see God's power break into your life in a powerful way.

On the next page is a preliminary inventory that will help you set the stage for these seven studies.

About the Authors

Lynn R. Buzzard was the executive director of the Christian Legal Society from 1971-1985. He is now a professor of law at Campbell University School of Law, Buies Creek, North Carolina. His wife, Juanita, served as education director at Western Springs Baptist Church. The late Laury Eck served as national coordinator of the Christian Conciliation Service of the Christian Legal Society from 1980-1986.

©1982, 1987, 1988, 1992 Christian Legal Society

ISBN: 0-944561-18-7

Founded in 1961, the Christian Legal Society (CLS) is a fellowship of Christian attorneys, judges, law professors and law students committed to integrating the Lordship of Christ with their professional responsibilities. In addition to sponsoring a conciliation ministry, the Society is active in religious liberty issues, encourages legal assistance for the under-represented, sponsors conferences and prepares publications.

For further information and resources on Christian conciliation, please contact the Association of Christian Conciliation Services, 1537 Avenue D, Suite 352, Billings, Montana 59102; telephone (406) 256-1583.

⊐|← INVENTORY
Conflict History: A Personal Evaluation

● *Briefly summarize the conflict as you perceive it–placing events in chronological order as much as possible.*

_____

_____

_____

_____

_____

_____

_____

_____

_____

_____

_____

_____

_____

_____

_____

_____

_____

_____

_____

● *Place a check by the following elements this conflict includes; cross out those it definitely does not include.*

_____Disagreements as to facts

_____Disagreements as to the "rightness" or propriety of certain actions.

_____Disagreements as to the requirements of the civil or criminal law.

_____Disagreements as to Biblical principles.

_____Personal feelings of hurt, anger, loss or guilt.

● *Write a brief comment in each space below indicating what effect this conflict is having in your life:*

On your attitudes: (e.g., resentment, bitterness)

_____

On your emotional energies for your family and friends

_____

On your personal devotional life

_____

On your sense of joy and vitality

_____

On your outlook in life, e.g., thankfulness, hopefulness

_____

On your finances

_____

On your reputation in the community or church

_____

● *This conflict could have been substantially avoided or minimized if:*

I had. . . .

_____

_____

The other party had. . . .

_____

_____

_____

● *Check any of the following feelings which you have had during this conflict:*

_____angry	_____isolated
_____hurt	_____bitter
_____lonely	_____guilty
_____furious	_____wholesome
_____thankful	_____resentful
_____joyful	_____sick
_____peaceful	_____bouncy
_____jealous	_____forgiving
_____proud	_____dispair

● *How do you want to respond to this conflict: (Check your desired response)*

_____"just settle"
_____"run"
_____"win"
_____"reconcile"

● *Are you really ready for reconciliation: (Check those you are ready for)*

_____for honesty about problems and about feelings.
_____for openness about hurt and anger.
_____for forgiveness and love.

● *What is the very best conclusion you can imagine to this conflict?*

_____

_____

_____

_____

_____

_____

_____

Study 1
Scriptures:

Matthew 5:23-24

23. If it should happen therefore that while you are presenting your offering upon the altar, and right there you remember that your brother has any grievance against you,

24. Leave your offering there upon the altar, and first go and make peace with your brother, and then come back and present your offering.

II Corinthians 5:18

18. And all things have become new through God who has reconciled us to himself by Jesus Christ and has given to us the ministry of reconciliation;

Ephesians 2:11-22

11. Wherefore remember that you were Gentiles in the flesh from the beginning, differing from that which is called Circumcision, which is the work of the hands in the flesh.

12. At that time you were without Christ, being aliens to the customs of Israel and strangers to the covenants of the promise, without hope and without God in the world.

13. But now, through Jesus Christ, you who sometime were far off are brought near by the blood of Christ.

14. For he is our peace, who has made both one, and has broken down the wall of separation between them;

15. And he has abolished in his flesh the enmity, even the law of commandments continued in ordinances, that he may create, in his person from the two, a new man, thus making peace;

16. And he reconciled both in one body with God, and with his cross he destroyed the enmity;

17. And he came and preached peace to you who are far away and to those who are near.

18. Through him we both are able to draw near by one Spirit to the Father.

19. Thus from hence forth you are neither strangers nor foreigners, but fellow-citizens with the saints and children of the house hold of God;

20. And you are built upon the foundation of the apostles and prophets, Jesus Christ himself being the cornerstone of the building:

21. And through him the whole building is fashioned and grows into a holy temple through the help of the Lord;

22. You also are builded by him for a habitation of God through the Spirit.

Study 1
RECONCILIATION

Scriptures:

Matthew 5:23-24
- *What is a prerequisite for worship?*

_____

II Corinthians 5:18
- *Describe Jesus' role as a peacemaker:*

For your meditation:

- *How much was God willing to INVEST in breaking down the barriers so that man and God could be reconciled? How much was he willing to RISK? to GIVE? What does reconciliation mean? Is it just forgiveness, or absence of conflict? What is the goal of reconciliation?*

Complete these questions/exercises:

- *In the chart below, begin by writing your own definition of reconciliation, and then listing 3 synonyms or words/phrases which describe what you believe "reconcile" means, e.g. "brought together"; and then five antonyms, or opposites, of reconciliation.*

Definition of Reconciliation:	
Synonyms	**Antonyms**
1._____	1._____
2._____	2._____
3._____	3._____
4._____	4._____
5._____	5._____

• Draw two symbols/pictures—a sort of before and after reconciliation. On the left symbolize the opposite of reconciled, on the right a picture symbolizing reconciled.

Alienation	Reconciliation

• Imagine the distance between the left and right of your symbols is 100 miles; that is, 100 miles represents the distance to travel between total alienation and full reconciliation. How many miles now exist do you think between you and the one with whom you are in conflict?

_____

• How far are you willing to travel?

_____

• What would be a first step you could take toward reconciliation?

_____

_____

_____

• How would your relationship with the other person be different if you were reconciled?

_____

_____

_____

• Are you willing to put reconciliation ahead of "winning"?

_____

_____

_____

● *Name at least one person who has had a ministry of reconciliation with you in this conflict?*

_____

_____

_____

Prayer: Lord Jesus, you gave your life to reconcile me to you, to bring me into your life and family. You suffered to win me as a friend. You died to win me as a child of God. Thank you Lord for breaking down the barriers and entering my life. Help me Lord in this conflict to seek to be reconciled. Forgive my closedmindedness and resentments. Open channels and doors. Destroy walls. Build Bridges. Give me the capacity to want to restore and build a relationship of love and care. Through Jesus, the Reconciler, Amen.

Study 2
Scriptures:

Psalm 133:1

1. Behold, how good and how pleasant it is for brethren to dwell together in unity!

John 17:11, 21-23
11. Hereafter I am not in the world, but these are in the world; and I am coming to thee. O holy Father, protect them in they name, which thou hast given me, that they may be one, even as we are.
21. So that they all may be one; just as thou, my Father, art with me, and I am with thee, that they also may be one with us; so that the world may believe that thou didst send me.
22. And the glory which thou gavest me, I gave to them; so that they may be one just as we are one.
23. I with them and thou with me, hat they may become perfected in one; so that the world may know that thou didst send me, and that thou didst love them just as thou didst love me.

Ephesians 1:19-21

19. And what is the exceeding greatness of his power in us as the result of the things we believe, according to the skill of his mighty power.
20. Which he wrought through Christ when he raised him from the dead and set him at his own right hand in heaven.
21. Far above all angels and power and might and dominion and every name that is named, not only in this world but also in the world which is to come.

Study 2
UNITY OF THE BODY OF CHRIST

Scriptures:

Psalm 133:1
John 17:11, 21-23
Ephesians 1:19-21

- *From these texts list four descriptive phrases which describe the believing community:*

1. _____
2. _____
3. _____
4. _____

For Meditation:

- *Why is the unity of the body of Christ so important to our Lord? What is it he is trying to create in his people that makes unity so central? If unity does not mean identity, but rather acknowledges differences and varieties of gifts, in what does the unity consist? How is it manifested?*

Complete these questions/exercises

- *Are the parties to this conflict part of God's family, those he wants to dwell in unity?*

_____
_____

- *Name four things you have in common with the other parties which can be emphasized as elements of your unity.*

1. _____
2. _____
3. _____
4. _____

● *Write in your own modern version, I Corinthians 1:10*

_____

_____

_____

_____

_____

_____

_____

_____

_____

_____

_____

_____

_____

_____

_____

_____

_____

_____

_____

_____

● *How can the way we deal with this conflict demonstrate and enhance the unity of the body?*

_____

_____

_____

_____

● *How has the community of believers been affected by this dispute? Has the unity increased or decreased?*

_____

_____

_____

_____

● *What possible consequences of this dispute could destroy our unity?*

_____

_____

_____

● *If you have had a history of relationships with the other party, list two good memories of those times–some positive moments.*

_____

_____

_____

_____

_____

● *Rank order these values:*

_____financial success

_____vindication

_____clarifying "rights"

_____legality

_____unity

_____justice

_____peace

_____forgiveness

Memory Verse:

"Let the peace of God rule in your hearts, to the which you are also called in one body" Col. 3:15.

"We are members one of another" Eph. 4:25.

Prayer: Lord Jesus, I know you are making a new people bound together with each other in love and care. I know you are creating a family and both the one I am in conflict with and I am in that family. I don't sense unity now, but division and tension. Lord, bring us together, take our hands and press them toward each other. Help us to discover how very much we have in common. And may this unity help us to find a way that resolves this dispute which builds an even greater bond.

Study 3
Scriptures:

1 John 1:8,9

    8. If we say that we have no sin, we deceive ourselves and the truth is not in us.

    9. If we confess our sins, he is faithful and just to forgive us our sins and to cleanse us from all our unrighteousness.

Psalm 34:14, 18

    14. Depart from evil and do good; seek peace and pursue it.

    18. The Lord is near to them that are brokenhearted, and he saves those who are humble in spirit.

Psalm 51:1-17

1. Have mercy upon me, O God, according to thy lovingkindness; according to the multitude of they tender mercies blot out my sins.
2. Wash me thoroughly from mine iniquity, and cleanse me from my sin;
3. For I acknowledge my transgressions, and my sin is ever before me.
4. Against thee, thee only, have I sinned, and done that which is evil in thy sight; for thou wilt be justified in they reproof, triumphant in thy judgments.
5. For behold, I was formed in iniquity and in sin did my mother conceive me.
6. Behold, thou desirest truth, and the hidden things of thy wisdom thou hast made known to me.
7. Sprinkle me with hyssop, and I shall be clean; wash me, and I shall be whiter than snow.
8. Satisfy me with thy joy and gladness, that my broken spirit may rejoice.
9. Turn they face away from my sins, and blot out all mine iniquities.
10. Create in me a clean heart, O God, and renew a right spirit within me.
11. Cast me not away from they presence; and take not thy holy spirit from me.
12. Restore to me the joy of thy salvation; and uphold me with thy glorious spirit,
13. Then will I teach transgressors they way, and sinners shall be converted unto thee.
14. Deliver me from bloodshedding, O God, thou God of my salvation, and my tongue shall sing aloud of thy righteousness.
15. O Lord, open thou my lips, and my mouth shall show forth thy praise;
16. For thou desirest not sacrifice; thou delightest not in burnt offerings.
17. The sacrifices of God are a broken spirit; a broken and a contrite heart, O God, thou wilt not despise.

Study 3
SIN AND CONFESSION

Scriptures:

I John 1:8,9
Psalm 34:14,18

● *List under the headings below the teachings of these texts regarding GOD'S ACTION, and OUR ACTION:*

God's Action	Our Action

Psalm 51:1-17

● *List what the Psalmist wants from God:*

_____
_____
_____
_____

● *List what the Psalmist says about himself:*

_____
_____
_____
_____

For Meditation:

If sin is falling short of God's glory and his will for our life, then it probably infects our lives even in ways of which we are not concious. Sin consists not only in outright evilness, but in unwillingness to obey, refusals to grow, resistance to the promptings of the spirit.

Complete these questions/exercises:

Make a quick list of 10 sins

_____

_____

_____

_____

_____

_____

_____

_____

_____

_____

- *Examine your list above. How many are things you DO? (Place a + by them.) How many are attitudes? (Circle them.)   How many focus on relationships? (Place a check by them.)   Which are usually causes of conflict?   Which tend to be exacerbated by conflict?   Place an * by any which are related to this conflict.*

- *Has sin in your life contributed to the cause of this dispute? Name some specific shortcomings.*

_____

_____

_____

_____

_____

_____

_____

_____

_____

_____

- *How has sin been a consequence of this dispute, e.g., attitudes, relationships?*

- *Is there an area of victory for you in your spiritual life, an area of growth which can be achieved through this conflict by confession and repentance? Identify it.*

- *Have you risked confession not only to God, but to your enemies and opponents?*

☐ Yes
☐ No

- *Are there spiritual problems in your life now which keep God from really displaying his grace in this conflict? Are you willing to open your life to grace?*

☐ Yes
☐ No

Memory Verse:

"Let all bitterness and wrath and anger and clamor and slander be put away from you, with all malice." Ephesians 4:31

Prayer: Dear Lord, I confess I am a sinner. My ego and pride get in the way of joy and life. My self-centeredness prevents the Spirit from flowing in my life. I focus on the faults of others, I expect others to change. Help me to be open to change. Help me to repent and be a new creation in Jesus. I release my pettiness, my securities and my agenda to your care and will. In Christ's name I pray this, Amen.

Study 4
Scriptures

Proverbs 24:17, 29

17. Do not rejoice when your enemy falls, and let not your heart be glad when he is overthrown.

29. Say not, I will do so to him as he has done to me; I will render to him according to his works.

Matthew 5: 7, 39-46

7. Blessed are the merciful, for they shall have mercy.

39. But I say to you that you should not resist evil; but whoever strikes you on your right cheek, turn to him the other also.

40. And if anyone wishes to sue you at the court and take away your shirt, let him have your robe also.

41. Whoever compels you to carry a burden for a mile, go with him two.

42. Whoever asks from you, give him; and whoever wishes to borrow from you, do not refuse him.

43. You have heard that it is said, Be kind to your friend, and hate your enemy.

44. But I say to you, Love your enemies, bless anyone who curses you, and pray for those who carry you away by force and persecute you,

45. So that you may become sons of your Father who is in heaven, who causes his sun to shine upon the good and the bad, and who pours down his rain upon the just and the unjust.

46. For if you love only those who love you, what reward will you have? Do not even the tax collectors do the same thing.

Colossians 3: 13

13. Forbearing one another, and forgiving one another; and if any one has a complaint against his fellow man, just as Christ forgave you, so should you also forgive.

I Peter 3: 9

9. Not rendering evil for evil, nor railing for railing, but instead of these render blessing for to this end you have been called, that you may inherit a blessing.

Romans 12:18-21

18. If it be possible, as much as lies in you live peaceably with all men.

19. Dearly beloved, avenge not yourselves, but rather restrain your wrath; for it is written, Vengeance is mine; I will execute justice for you, said the Lord.

20. Therefore if your enemy hunger, feed him; if he thirst, give him drink; for in so doing, you shall heap coals of fire on his head.

Be not overcome by evil, but overcome evil with good.

Matt. 18:21-35

21. ¶Then Peter came up and said to him, My Lord, if my brother is at fault with me, how many times should I forgive him? up to seven times?

22. Jesus said to him, I do not say to you up to seven times, but up to seventy times seventy-seven.

23. ¶Therefore the kingdom of heaven is likened to a king who wanted to take an accounting from his servants.

24. And when he began to take the accounting, they brought to him one who owed ten thousand talents.

And as he could not pay, his lord commanded him to be sold, together with his wife and children and all that he had, so that he could pay.

The servant then fell down, worshipped him and said, My lord, have patience with me and I will pay you everything.

27. Then the master of that servant had pity, so he released him and cancelled his debt.

28. But that servant went out, and found one of his fellow servants, who owed him a hundred pennies; and he seized him and tried to choke him, saying to him, Give me what you owe me.

29. So his fellow servant fell down at his feet, and begged him, saying, Have patience with me and I will pay you.

30. But he was not willing; and he went and had him put into prison until he should pay him what he owed him.

31. When their fellow servants saw what had happened, they were sorry, and came and informed their master of everything that had happened.

32. Then his master called him and said to him. O wicked servant, I cancelled all your debt because you begged me.

33. Was it not right for you to have mercy on your fellow servant, just as I had mercy on you?

34. So his master was angry, and delivered him to the scourgers until he should pay everything he owed him.

35. So will my Father in heaven do to you, if you do not forgive each man his brother's fault from your hearts.

Study 4
FORGIVENESS

Scriptures:

Proverbs 24:17,29
Matthew 5:7, 39-46
Matthew 18:21-35
Romans 12:18-21
Colossians 3:13
I Peter 3:9

● *Look in these texts for attitudes of the believer toward the wrongdoer. List 10 below:*

1. _____
2. _____
3. _____
4. _____
5. _____
6. _____
7. _____
8. _____
9. _____
10. _____

Complete these questions/exercises:

● *Indicate 3 times in your life when others have forgiven you and accepted and loved you?*

1. _____

2. _____

3. _____

● *What is the difference between forgiveness and just avoidance?*

_____
_____
_____

- *List 4 antonyms/opposites of forgiveness:*

     1. _____

     2. _____

     3. _____

     4. _____

- *Which do you think is harder, to GIVE forgiveness, or to RECEIVE forgiveness? Why?*

  _____

  _____

  _____

- *In this dispute, what action of others COULD you choose to forgive?*

  _____

  _____

  _____

- *In this dispute, of what do YOU need forgiveness from others?*

  _____

  _____

  _____

- *Have you specifically asked forgiveness from anyone in regard to your role in this dispute? What was the response?*

  _____

  _____

  _____

● *Should we ever ask forgiveness if we think we have done nothing wrong but others believe we have and hold resentments? Does asking forgiveness imply guilt?*

_____

_____

_____

_____

Memory Verse:

"And be kind to one another, tenderhearted, forgiving one another, as God in Christ forgave you." Ephesians 4:32

Prayer: Lord Jesus; thank you for setting me free by forgiving me. Lord I have been hurt, I feel like a victim, and its hard to forgive. It's hard for me to let go of my anger. I am hiding it inside me and storing it up. Lord, give me such a perception of your love for me, that I can truly give to others the freedom you have given me through forgiveness. And help me to accept the forgiveness others offer me, so that I may be released from guilt and open to new joy with you and your children. Amen.

Study 5
Scriptures:

1 John 4: 12-21

12. No man has seen God at any time. If we love one another, God abides in us, and his love is perfected in us;

13. Hereby we know that we abide in him and he in us, because he has given us his spirit.

14. And we have seen and do testify that the Father sent his Son to be the Saviour of the world.

15. Whoever shall confess that Jesus is the Son of God, God abides in him and he in God.

16. And we have believed and have known the love that God has for us. God is love; and he who dwells in love abides in God.

17. Herein is his love made perfect in us, so that we may have boldness in us, so that we may have goodness in the day of judgment; because as he is, so are we in this world.

18. There is no fear in love; but perfect love casts out fear, because fear is tormenting. He who fears is not made perfect in love.

19. We love God because he first loved us.

20. If a man says, I love God, and yet hates his brother, he is a liar; for he who does not love his brother whom he has seen, how can he love God whom he has not seen?

21. And this commandment we have received from him, That he who loves God ought to love his brother also.

1 John 3: 17, 18

17. Whoever has worldly goods and sees his brother in need and shuts his mercy from him, how can the love of God dwell in him.

18. My children, let us not love one another in word and in tongue, but in deed and in truth.

1 Corinthians 13: 4-7

4. Love is long-suffering and kind; love does not envy; love does not make a vain display of itself, and does not boast.

5. Does not behave itself unseemly, seeks not its own, is not easily provoked, thinks no evil;

6. Rejoices not over iniquity, but rejoices in the truth;

7. Bears all things, believes all things, hopes all things, endures all things.

 **Study 5
LOVE**

Scripture:

**I John 4:12-21
I John 3:17,18
I Corinthians 13:4-7**

- *What does each verse teach about the relationship of love to another believer:*

    I John 4:12-21

    _____

    _____

    I John 3:17,18

    _____

    _____

    I Corinthians 13:4-7

    _____

    _____

Complete these questions/exercises:

- *Write a paraphrase of I Corinthians 13:4-7*

    _____

    _____

    _____

    _____

    _____

    _____

    _____

    _____

    _____

    _____

    _____

● *Verse 7 refers to "bearing," "believing," "hoping" and "enduring" "all things!" In the four columns below list a couple of things that in this conflict Christ is calling you to bear, believe, hope for, and endure.*

Bearing	Believing	Hoping	Enduring

● *For each of the items in the column, give yourself a + for the items you are doing pretty well at. Circle two really difficult ones for you right now. Pray right now for God's strength in those two areas.*

● *List three ways you may actively love someone even if they don't love you.*

1. _____

2. _____

3. _____

In which of the following ways are you manifesting God's will that you love the one with whom you are in conflict?

_____Praying for them regularly and positively.
_____Thinking the best of them, not assuming the worst.
_____Focusing on some loving action you can take, not on your feelings.

Memory Verse

"And we know that all things work together for good to them that love God" Romans 8:28.

Study 6
Scriptures:

Matthew 18: 15-20

15. Now then if your brother sins against you, go and rebuke him alone; if he listens to you, then you have won your brother.

16. But if he will not listen to you take one or two with you, because at the mouth of two or three witnesses every word is established.

17. And if he will not listen to them, tell the congregation; and if he will not listen to the congregation, then regard him as a tax collector and a heathen.

18. Truly I say to you, Whatever you bind on earth will be bound in heaven, and whatever you release on earth will be released in heaven.

19. Again I say to you that if two of you are worthy on earth, anything that they would ask will be done for them by my Father in heaven.

20. For wherever two or three are gathered in my name I am there among them.

Ephesians 4: 11-16

11. And he has assigned some as apostles and some as prophets and some as evangelists and some as pastors and some as teachers;

12. For the perfecting of the saints for the work of the ministry, for the edifying of the body of Christ,

13. Until we all become one in faith and in the knowledge of the Son of God, and become a perfect man according to the measure of the stature of the fulness of Christ,

14. That we henceforth be not as children easily stirred and carried away by every wind of false doctrines of men, who through their craftiness are artful in deceiving the people;

15. But that we be sincere in our love, so that in everything we may progress through Christ who is the head.

16. It is through him that the whole body is closely and firmly united at all joints, according to the measure of the gift which is given to every member, for the guidance and control of the body, in order to complete the edifying of the body in love.

Study 6
TELL IT TO THE CHURCH

Scriptures:
   Matthew 18:15-20
   Ephesians 4:11-16

Complete these questions/exercises:

- *List the three steps Jesus outlines in Matthew 18:15ff for resolving disputes*

   1. _____
   2. _____
   3. _____

- *What reasons does Paul list in I Corinthians 6 for the church to be involved in disputes?*

   _____
   _____
   _____

- *What gifts and perspectives do you believe the church possesses that can be healing of conflict?*

   _____
   _____
   _____
   _____

- *Name one person you know who is an effective peacemaker/healer?*

_____

- *What persons in the church (fellow believers) have you consulted regarding this dispute? What suggestions have they made?*

_____

_____

_____

_____

- *If you are willing to let the church fulfill the mandate of Matthew 18 and I Corinthians 6, and abide by the decision, read and sign the covenant below:*

> Whereas I have committed my life to Jesus Christ and to obey his teaching and to find my peace and righteousness only in Him; and whereas I have also committed my life to the church, his family of my brothers and sisters with whom I have oneness and fellowship; and whereas I believe He has called us to claim the gifts of wisdom and discernment in the body and to accept the counsel of our spiritual family, I am willing to follow the mandates of I Corinthians 6 and Matthew 18 and to abide by the decision of the church.
>
> Date _____

Signed _____

Memory Verse:

"Brethren, if a man be overtaken in a fault, ye which are spiritual, restore such a one in the spirit of meekness; considering thyself, lest thou also be tempted? Galatians 6:1

Study 7
Scriptures:

Matthew 5:9

9. Blessed are the peacemakers, for they shall be called sons of God.

Romans 12:18

18. If it be possible, as much as lies in you, live peaceably with all men.

I Thessalonians 5:13

13. That you esteem them very highly in love, and be at peace with them for their work's sake.

James 3: 17, 18

17. But the wisdom that is from above is first pure then full of peace, and is gentle, obedient, full of mercy and good fruits, without partiality and without hypocrisy.

18. And the fruit of righteousness is sown in peace by the peacemakers.

Study 7
PEACE

Scriptures:
    Matthew 5:9
    Romans 12:18
    I Thess 5:13
    James 3:17,18

Complete these questions/exercises:

- *List in the diagram below five attributes/qualities of a "peaceful" spiritual life, and five opposites of peace.*

Peace	UnPeace
1._____	1._____
2._____	2._____
3._____	3._____
4._____	4._____
5._____	5._____

- *How Can God give us peace in the midst of trial/temptation/conflict? Suggest a couple of things.*

- *What actions on our part are destructive of peace?*

    _____
    _____
    _____

- *Create a symbolic collage of peace, placing some symbol in each portion of the image below.*

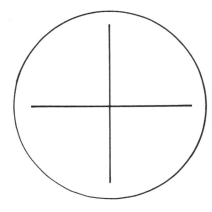

- *Draw a graph which represents the degree of peace vs. non-peace in your life during the course of this conflict. Put some key words at the peaks and valleys to indicate the events which created these extremes.*

peace

Unpeace

- *What is one thing you can do to help create peace in this relationship?*

_____

_____

_____

Memory Verses:

"Thou wilt keep him in perfect peace whose mind is stayed on thee: because he trusteth in thee." Isa. 26:3.

"Let the peace of Christ rule in your hearts, since as members of one body you were called to peace. And be thankful." Colossians 3:15

# WHAT NOW—READY FOR RECONCILIATION?

In the light of the previous studies, answer the following questions:

- *The thing God wants me to learn from this conflict is:*

  _____
  _____
  _____
  _____

- *This conflict offers an opportunity for. . . .*

  _____
  _____
  _____
  _____

- *The next step that I believe God is calling on me to take in regard to this dispute is:*

  _____
  _____
  _____
  _____

- *I will know Christ has been present in this situation if some of the following is evident/happens:*

  _____
  _____
  _____
  _____
  _____
  _____
  _____
  _____

DATE DUE

	MY 2'96			
	9/1 4:31			
	SE 29 '00			

● *To which of* **JY 24 02**

_____I am				onored.
_____I car				ness.
_____I am				
_____I am				
_____I am				
_____I car				t is wrong.
_____I am				
_____I am love				honestly with truth and

DEMCO 38-297